OFFICIAL

Cambridge English

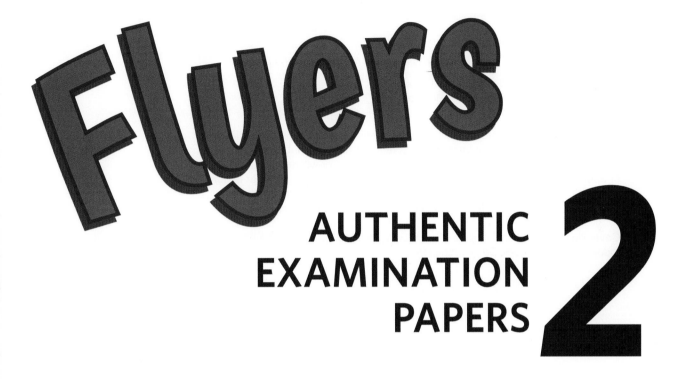

Flyers

AUTHENTIC EXAMINATION PAPERS **2**

T0349718

STUDENT'S BOOK

Cambridge University Press
www.cambridge.org/elt

Cambridge Assessment English
www.cambridgeenglish.org

Information on this title: www.cambridge.org/9781316636251

© Cambridge University Press and UCLES 2018

First published 2018

20 19 18 17 16 15 14 13

Printed in Poland by Opolgraf

A catalogue record for this publication is available from the British Library

ISBN 978-1-316-63625-1 Student's Book
ISBN 978-1-316-63628-2 Answer Booklet
ISBN 978-1-316-63631-2 Audio CD

Cover illustration: (camel) nojman/iStock/Getty Images Plus; (ball) MuchMania/iStock/Getty Images Plus;
(books) adekvat/iStock/Getty Images Plus

Contents

Part 1
– 5 questions –

Listen and draw lines. There is one example.

Helen   Michael   Holly   Robert

William   Betty   David

Part 2

– 5 questions –

Listen and write. There is one example.

<u>Castle visit</u>

	Day of visit:	..........Wednesday..........
1	Name of castle:	.....................Castle
2	When people lived there:	....................years ago
3	Name of film:	Brave and ....
4	Katy wants to wear:	a ....
5	Meet in car park at the:	....

Part 3
– 5 questions –

Which creature did each child in Mr White's class draw?

Listen and write a letter in each box. There is one example.

George   H

Richard   ☐

John   ☐

Sarah   ☐

Emma   ☐

Daisy   ☐

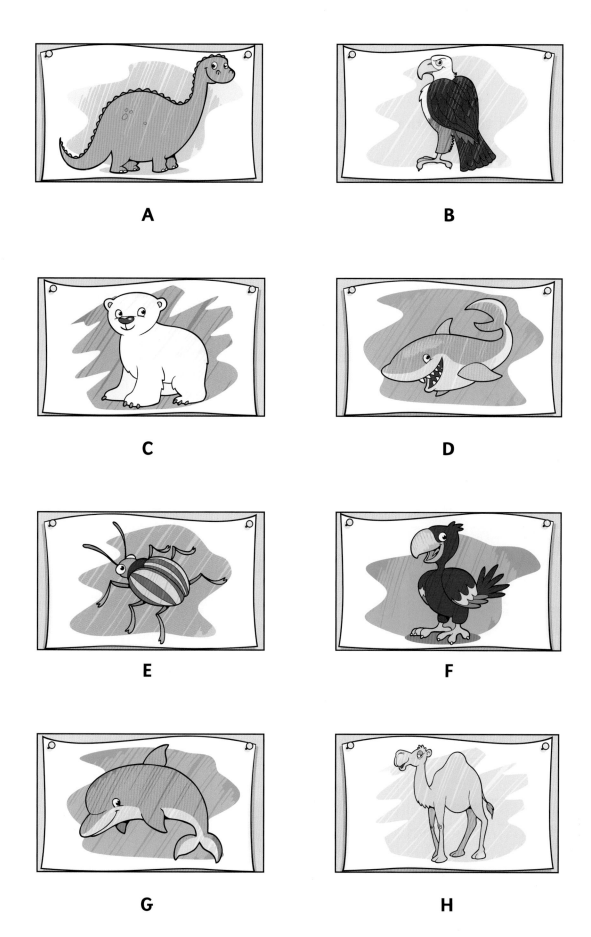

A

B

C

D

E

F

G

H

Part 4
– 5 questions –

Listen and tick (✔) the box. There is one example.

How are Charlie and his mum going to get to the city?

A ✔   B ☐   C ☐

1 Where are they going to go first?

A ☐   B ☐   C ☐

2 What is Mum going to buy?

A ☐   B ☐   C ☐

3 What are they going to have for lunch?

A ☐   B ☐   C ☐

4 Where are they going to go in the evening?

A ☐   B ☐   C ☐

5 Who is going to meet Mum and Charlie in the evening?

A ☐   B ☐   C ☐

Part 5
– 5 questions –

Listen and colour and write. There is one example.

Reading and Writing

Part 1

– 10 questions –

Look and read. Choose the correct words and write them on the lines. There is one example.

golf   channels   a mechanic   a museum

a theatre

a race

an artist

a university

a pilot   a quiz   cartoons

If your car engine is making a strange noise, call this person!	**a mechanic**	an astronaut
1 People wear costumes and act on a stage here and you can come and watch.	....	
2 When you go to a restaurant, this person carries your plate of food to you.	....	
3 You answer questions in this and the person with the most correct answers might get a prize!	....	a factory
4 Two people play this game on a board that has black and white squares on it.	....	
5 This brave person learns to fly in a rocket and travel through space.	....	
6 These are drawings or short films that usually make you laugh.	....	a waiter
7 Older students come to this place when they have left school. They can study special subjects here.	....	
8 In this sport, you hit a small hard ball into a hole that has a flag next to it.	....	chess
9 The people that work here might make things out of metal or plastic or wood.	....	
10 You can change these to watch different programmes on your television.	....	

Part 2

– 5 questions –

Helen is talking to George about a festival. What does George say?

Read the conversation and choose the best answer.
Write a letter (A–H) for each answer.

You do not need to use all the letters. There is one example.

Example
Helen: Hello, George. Did your parents take you to the music festival last week?
George: .... C ....

Questions

1 **Helen:** Who did you go to the festival with?

   George: ....

2 **Helen:** What was the festival like?

   George: ....

3 **Helen:** Which was the best band at the festival?

   George: ....

4 **Helen:** Were there any kids from our class at the festival?

   George: ....

5 **Helen:** Are you going to put some photos online?

   George: ....

A	That's a good idea. I'll do that now!
B	Most of them were great but The Pond was perhaps my favourite.
C	Actually, they couldn't go this time. **(Example)**
D	I'm going to go back to school tomorrow.
E	Excellent! Really good fun.
F	I didn't see anyone I knew, actually, but I think Harry was there somewhere.
G	That's right, I felt really excited about having guitar lessons.
H	My uncle had tickets, so I went with him and my cousins.

Part 3
– 6 questions –

Read the story. Choose a word from the box. Write the correct word next to numbers 1–5. There is one example.

Example				
team	arrived	lazy	term	match
sure	believed	fell	member	score

David and Emma are in the basketball .... *team* .... but during the practice last Thursday, David **(1)** .... over and hurt his knee.

'The doctor says I can't play in the next three matches,' David told his sports teacher. 'Sorry!'

'No problem,' the teacher said. 'Who might play instead? Do you know anyone?'

'Frank Point is a year younger than us, but he's really tall and he's played very well in the playground this **(2)** .... You could ask him,' David answered.

Frank wasn't **(3)** .... about playing in the match.

'I'm not as good as Emma and the others,' he told the teacher, 'but I'll try.'

When the players from Bridge School **(4)** .... , Frank
felt worried, but he soon began to really enjoy the game.
His team won! Frank got four goals and the **(5)** ....
at the end of the match was 55 to 32. 'We'd like you to play for us every
week until David is better!' the teacher said. 'Woooooow! Great! Yes,
if you want!' Frank said.

(6) Now choose the best name for the story.

Tick one box.

Emma's basketball game ☐

David's game is improving ☐

Frank's important match ☐

Part 4

– 10 questions –

Read the text. Choose the right words and write them on the lines.

Swans

Example Swans are .... the .... largest birds in the duck

1 family. There are six different kinds .... swans

which have white bodies, but in a few parts of the world there are

black swans too. Swans are clever and remember people who have

2 .... kind or unkind to them! A frightened

3 .... really angry swan can break a man's leg

4 .... its strong wings!

Swans live on rivers and lakes. But in the winter months, some

might live near the sea because salt water is usually a little

5 .... than river water. Swans don't usually fly

6 very far from the place .... they build their

nests. It takes between 35 and 42 days for a baby swan, which

7 .... called a 'cygnet', to break open its egg!

8 A baby swan can be grey .... white. Wild swans

usually live for about seven years, but some live a lot longer. A swan

9 eats underwater plants. It finds these by .... its

long neck deep into the water and its tail up into the air! Swans might

10 .... eat small frogs and insects.

Example	the	a	one
1	of	up	off
2	be	been	being
3	or	because	while
4	out	at	with
5	warm	warmer	warmest
6	who	if	where
7	are	is	was
8	not	nowhere	no
9	puts	put	putting
10	ever	also	yet

Part 5

– 7 questions –

Look at the picture and read the story. Write some words to complete the sentences about the story. You can use 1, 2, 3 or 4 words.

Katy and Michael's app

Katy and Michael both enjoy playing computer games. Last summer they talked a lot about designing online games and apps, as well. In the future, they both want to be designers like their father.

In the autumn, they decided to design an app to help kids choose comics or story books. They agreed about something important. Children must enjoy using the app. It mustn't be boring.

'Well, we could make something appear on the screen each time they choose a book,' Michael said.

'OK! What about a really strange creature that hops across the screen, or perhaps we could show rain that changes into a rainbow?'

'Brilliant!' said Michael. 'Shall we ask Dad about this?' 'Yes, let's ask him now,' said Katy.

Their father loved the idea. 'Here's an amazing program,' he said. 'You can use it to make your app. And don't worry. I can help.'

Last month Katy and Michael's app appeared online for the first time! A journalist who wrote for a computer magazine called them about it.

'I'd like to write about you in the magazine. Which do you enjoy most, now?' he asked. 'Designing apps or playing games?'

'Designing apps!' Katy and Michael answered.

'OK! And I'll need a photo of you. Can we come round and take one?'

'You don't have to do that!' Katy laughed. 'We'll text you one!'

Examples

Katy and Michael are very interested in making <u>online games and apps</u>.

The children would like to be .... <u>designers</u> .... in the future, like their father.

Questions

1   They wanted to design an app which helped children choose stories and .... to read.

2   They didn't want the app to be ....

3   Katy and Michael wanted the app to show something funny like a .... that moves or a rainbow.

4   They decided to tell .... about their idea.

5   The children used .... to design their app.

6   A journalist who worked .... phoned them when he heard about their app.

7   The children now think .... is more fun than playing computer games.

Part 6

– 5 questions –

Read the diary and write the missing words. Write one word on each line.

Example	We tried ....*to*.......... cycle up Fairgreen Hill
	but soon got off and pushed our bikes up the hill instead!
1	We .... really thirsty at the top because it
2	was a hot day so we .... all the lemonade
	and water we had with us. Then we ate two huge sandwiches and
3	.... on the ground and chatted for about an
	hour. Cycling back down was much easier. But I went too fast
	when we cycled back down and now I've got a problem with one
4	.... my wheels.
5	I'll fix .... tomorrow.

Part 7

Look at the three pictures. Write about this story. Write 20 or more words.

....

....

....

....

....

Listening

Part 1
– 5 questions –

Listen and draw lines. There is one example.

Harry   Richard   Emma   George

Katy   Robert   Sophia

Part 2

– 5 questions –

Listen and write. There is one example.

My favourite pop star!

Age at first singing lesson: ....10...................

1   Favourite song: ....

2   Where she enjoys singing most: at ....

3   Manager's name: Michael ....

4   Before going on stage, has: some ....

5   Favourite thing she wears: her ....

Part 3
– 5 questions –

Where did Frank's mother see each thing?

Listen and write a letter in each box. There is one example.

	taxi	G
	rocket	☐
	fire engine	☐
	ambulance	☐
	bicycle	☐
	spaceship	☐

A

B

C

D

E

F

G

H

Part 4

– 5 questions –

Listen and tick (✔) the box. There is one example.

What time will Oliver arrive at his cousin's house?

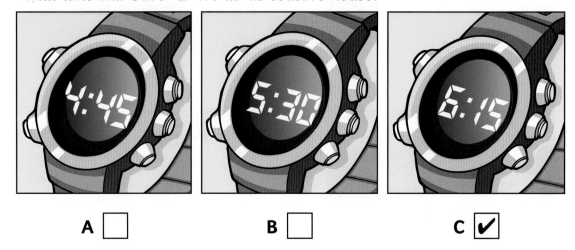

A ☐   B ☐   C ✔

1   What does Oliver hope to do?

A ☐   B ☐   C ☐

2   What has Oliver not found yet?

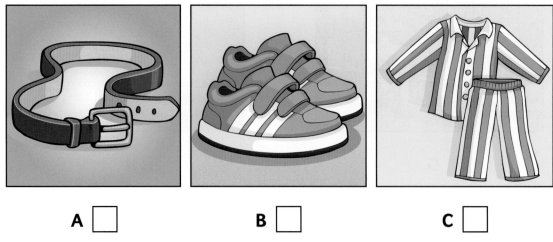

A ☐   B ☐   C ☐

3 Which homework will Oliver take?

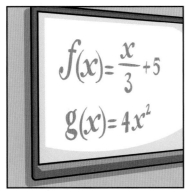

A ☐ B ☐ C ☐

4 What must Oliver remember to take?

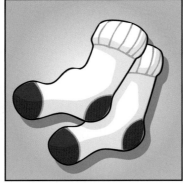

A ☐ B ☐ C ☐

5 Who must Oliver send a message to?

A ☐ B ☐ C ☐

Part 5

– 5 questions –

Listen and colour and write. There is one example.

Reading and Writing

Part 1
– 10 questions –

Look and read. Choose the correct words and write them on the lines. There is one example.

a chemist's   a project   a bin   an astronaut

a camel	insects

This person works in space and might travel to another planet.   an astronaut

1   This animal moves slowly and can hide its head and legs inside its hard shell.   ....

2   The people who work in this place make things like cars and computers.   ....

3   When you don't want to keep something, you throw it in this.   ....

4   Birds build this in a tree for their eggs and their babies.   ....

5   You can buy things like medicine, soap and shampoo in this place.   ....

6   This big animal can walk for a long time in hot, dry places. It can carry people or heavy things.   ....

7   You can use these when you want to cut paper or your hair.   ....

8   This person writes for newspapers or websites about things that have happened.   ....

9   People play games and do sport in this building   ....

10 Butterflies and beetles are examples of these. Bigger animals like frogs eat them.   ....

a gym   eagles

police officer   a tortoise

a factory   scissors

glue   a nest   a journalist

Part 2
– 5 questions –

Helen has started to learn to play the drums. What does Helen say to Katy?

Read the conversation and choose the best answer.
Write a letter (A–H) for each answer.

You do not need to use all the letters. There is one example.

Example

Katy:	When did you start having drum lessons?
Helen:	............................D............................

Questions

1   Katy: How often do you practise the drums?

    Helen: ....

2   Katy: Where do you practise the drums?

    Helen: ....

3   Katy: What is your drum teacher like?

    Helen: ....

4   Katy: I really like pop music.

    Helen: ....

5   Katy: Would you like to play drums in a band?

    Helen: ....

A	In the basement, because the drums are very noisy.
B	Because I haven't learnt that yet, actually.
C	He's an amazing drum player and very cool.
D	Last year. The drums were my birthday present. **(Example)**
E	Sure! But I don't know anyone else who plays an instrument.
F	No, they're at 5 o'clock on Mondays.
G	I should do it every day, but sometimes I forget.
H	Me too, but rock music is my favourite.

Part 3

– 6 questions –

Read the story. Choose a word from the box. Write the correct word next to numbers 1–5. There is one example.

Example				
entrance	worried	heard	silver	path
ago	tomorrow	dark	month	hid

Harry's class at school was learning about caves, so the geography teacher, Mrs Park, decided to take the class to visit one. They caught a special bus to the ....entrance............ of an enormous cave. There they had to put on helmets with torches on them because the cave was really **(1)** .... inside. Without torches they couldn't see anything. First, they went down some steps. Then they walked along a **(2)** .... and saw some interesting rocks. Mrs Park said, 'Many years **(3)** .... , pirates kept their treasure here. We might find some gold!' They arrived at a small lake, where some boats were waiting. Mrs Park said, 'These boats will take us to the exit of the cave.' Harry got into one of the boats, and saw something in the water. 'Look, I've found some **(4)** .... money.

I don't think a pirate **(5)** .... this money here! It's

very new!' said Harry. There was a shop near the bus stop. Harry used the

money to buy some sweets and ate them with his classmates.

(6) Now choose the best name for the story.

Tick one box.

Mrs Park drives a boat ☐

Harry finds the pirate's treasure ☐

The class explores a cave ☐

Part 4

– 10 questions –

Read the text. Choose the right words and write them on the lines.

Kites

Example	Kites have .... *been* .... popular for over two thousand years.
1	Some people think that the first kites were made ....
2	leaves from trees. Kites can be .... different
	shapes and sometimes they can look like animals or strange creatures.
	They can be really small or enormous. It is often difficult to fly a kite for
3	a long time .... there has to be enough wind.
4	It can take a lot of practice to learn to fly a kite ....
5	Kites are .... always toys for children. A lot of
6	grown-ups love flying .... too. There are special
	racing kites that people use in competitions. In some countries there are
7	huge kite festivals .... you can see hundreds of
	kites in the air at the same time.
8	Some clever people have also .... kites to learn
	more about the weather. They put special cameras on kites to help
9	.... find out about places that are too difficult or
10	dangerous to .... on the ground.

Example	be	been	being
1	in	of	up
2	many	any	every
3	because	while	if
4	else	well	ever
5	nothing	no	not
6	them	they	their
7	who	where	how
8	use	using	used
9	we	us	our
10	explore	exploring	explored

Part 5
– 7 questions –

Look at the picture and read the story. Write some words to complete the sentences about the story. You can use 1, 2, 3 or 4 words.

The golf ball

Richard and Emma are friends. One day, Richard said, 'Emma, would you like to play golf?' 'Yes,' said Emma. 'Let's go to the park by the river!' Emma was brilliant at golf, and the ball went a really long way when she hit it.

Richard and Emma saw the ball bounce once on the grass. Then they saw it fall into the river. 'Oh no!' said Emma.

The children saw a man who was fishing. 'Our golf ball went into the river. Can we borrow your net to get it, please?' asked Emma. The man agreed.

The children thanked the man, and went to find the ball. 'I can't see the ball from here,' Emma said. 'I know! If we stand up there on that bridge, we can see better,' said Emma. 'Good idea,' said Richard. 'Let's try!'

So they stood on the bridge and tried to get the ball with the net. Then Emma's hat fell off her head and into the river too!

But then a woman walked past with a friendly dog. Suddenly, the dog jumped into the water and fetched both the ball and the hat. The kids decided to stop playing golf and throw the ball for the dog instead, which was much more fun.

Examples

One day Richard invited ....*Emma*................ to play golf with him.

They decided to play in the park that was ....*by the river*.......... .

Questions

1   When Emma hit the ball, it went a very ....

2   The ball fell .... after it bounced once on
    the grass.

3   Richard and Emma borrowed a .... from a man
    who was fishing.

4   The children couldn't see the ball so they decided to go up on the

    ....

5   Emma lost .... in the water while they were
    trying to get the ball.

6   The woman's .... fetched the ball and the hat
    from the river.

7   Richard and Emma had .... throwing the ball
    than playing golf.

Part 6
– 5 questions –

Read the diary and write the missing words. Write one word on each line.

Tuesday

Today was a special day. We went out ....<u>to</u>..................

a restaurant for dinner because my sister Sarah won the first

1 .... in an art competition. Sarah chose

the restaurant too. The food was delicious and the waiters

2 .... very friendly!

3 On my birthday I am .... to go to a

restaurant too. I think I will choose the same one again, because

4 I .... like to go back there.

Now it's very late but I'm still awake because I have

5 .... so much food!

Example

Part 7

Look at the three pictures. Write about this story. Write 20 or more words.

....

....

....

....

....

Part 1

– 5 questions –

Listen and draw lines. There is one example.

Frank   Oliver   Sophia   Betty

David   Emma   George

Part 2

– 5 questions –

Listen and write. There is one example.

<u>Things I need to take to school</u>

	For walk:	.... *sunglasses* ....
1	For sports lessons:	white ....
2	For art class:	picture of ....
3	A file for:	.... projects
4	For camping:	'Blue ....' shampoo
5	For 'pets day':	....

41

Part 3

– 5 questions –

Which hobby does each of Richard's friends have?

Listen and write a letter in each box. There is one example.

	Harry	B
	Helen	☐
	Katy	☐
	Michael	☐
	William	☐
	Sarah	☐

A

B

C

D

E

F

G

H

Part 4

– 5 questions –

Listen and tick (✔) the box. There is one example.

What time will Sophia's family leave home tomorrow?

A ☐

B ☐

C ✔

1 What must Sophia put in her backpack tonight?

A ☐

B ☐

C ☐

2 Where is the hotel?

A ☐

B ☐

C ☐

3   Which new food will Sophia eat?

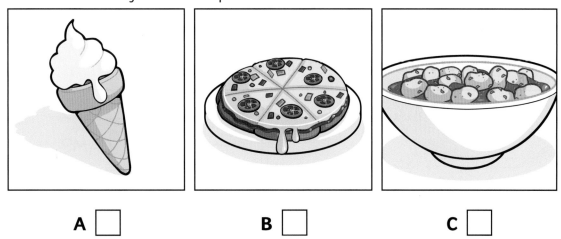

A ☐   B ☐   C ☐

4   What will the weather be like?

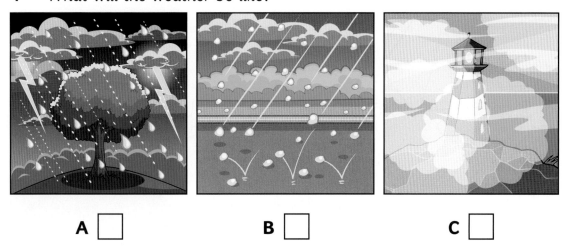

A ☐   B ☐   C ☐

5   What is Sophia going to do on holiday?

A ☐   B ☐   C ☐

Part 5
– 5 questions –

Listen and colour and write. There is one example.

Part 1

– 10 questions –

Look and read. Choose the correct words and write them on the lines. There is one example.

a designer   a university   a bridge   a journalist

a factory

the Earth

> A person with this job has ideas for making new things like clothes or cars. ...... *a designer*
>
> **1**   This is where you go to watch people act on stage. ....
>
> **2**   You go over this to cross a railway or road. ....
>
> **3**   It is this person's job to repair car engines and change tyres. ....
>
> **4**   People can save their money here or get it when they need it. ....
>
> **5**   This is a little river that you often find in the mountains. ....
>
> **6**   It's this person's job to write in newspapers about things that happen in the world. ....
>
> **7**   This is a place where older students study special subjects. ....
>
> **8**   You might find this inside a mountain and bats often live here. ....
>
> **9**   Animals like camels live in this place where the weather is often hot and dry. ....
>
> **10**   This person wears a uniform and might help with traffic problems. ....

a theatre

a stadium

a police officer

a mechanic

a bank

a manager

a desert   a cave   a stream

Part 2

– 5 questions –

William is talking to his grandmother about school. What does William say?

Read the conversation and choose the best answer.
Write a letter (A–H) for each answer.

You do not need to use all the letters. There is one example.

Example

	Grandma:	Did you have a good day at school, William?
	William:	.... B ....

Questions

1   **Grandma:**   Who did you play with in the break?

   William: ....

2   **Grandma:**   Which lesson did you enjoy the most?

   William: ....

3   **Grandma:**   You usually have a piano lesson today too, don't you?

   William: ....

4   **Grandma:**   Have you got to do lots of homework this evening?

   William: ....

5   **Grandma:**   Are you going on a school trip tomorrow?

   William: ....

A	Not yet, but I'm good at music.
B	Yes, thanks, it was brilliant. **(Example)**
C	I had a game of basketball with three of my friends.
D	OK. I'll go with Michael.
E	They were all interesting, actually.
F	Yes, to the castle. I hope we will have fun there.
G	That's right, every Wednesday after lunch.
H	Only a bit, just some maths.

Part 3
– 6 questions –

Read the story. Choose a word from the box. Write the correct word next to numbers 1–5. There is one example.

Example				
astronaut	thousands	excited	early	suddenly
air	wonderful	dark	unfriendly	creatures

Emma's dad was a pilot but he wanted to be an ....astronaut............. .

Emma loved listening to her father's funny stories about amazing planets

and the strange **(1)** .... that lived there.

One night, Emma couldn't sleep. She looked at all the stars through her

bedroom window. 'There are **(2)** .... of them,' she

thought.

'I really want to travel in space and meet an alien! One day, perhaps.'

Then **(3)** .... some lights appeared in the sky.

The lights came nearer and nearer. 'It's a spaceship!' Emma whispered.

'Woooow, it's in my garden now!' Emma ran outside but it was

(4) .... and difficult to see very well. Something with

a huge helmet on its head was opening a door and waving to her. Emma

began to laugh. She could see her father's face! 'Hello Emma,' he said.

'Do you like my **(5)** .... new helicopter? Come for

a ride in it! We might see a spaceship!'

(6)   Now choose the best name for the story.

Tick one box.

Emma's trip into space	☐
The scary alien	☐
Dad's surprise for Emma	☐

Part 4
– 10 questions –

Read the text. Choose the right words and write them on the lines.

X-rays

Example　When .... *someone* .... breaks an arm or leg, they need to

go to hospital to have an x-ray. An x-ray is a special kind of photo

1　.. helps doctors to see inside a person's body.

2　Dentists .... use x-ray machines to fix problems.

X-ray photos can show the dentist where there are any broken teeth or

3　teeth that have holes in .... A man called Wilhelm

4　Rontgen invented the x-ray machine .... the end

5　of the 19th century. The first x-ray that he ....

was of his wife's hand. Rontgen won prizes for his important new idea.

6　People used x-rays to help .... shoes in the middle

of the last century, too. They used the machine to help them choose the

7　.. shoes.

8　We .... find x-ray machines in shoe shops now,

9　but they are .... in airports. These machines look

10　inside rucksacks and .... bags that people take

on planes.

Example	someone	everything	anywhere
1	what	which	who
2	also	once	else
3	its	one	them
4	since	at	over
5	took	take	taken
6	sell	sold	selling
7	good	better	best
8	aren't	haven't	don't
9	most	usually	much
10	each	other	every

Part 5

– 7 questions –

Look at the picture and read the story. Write some words to complete the sentences about the story. You can use 1, 2, 3 or 4 words.

Snowboarding lesson

Before Sophia and Robert had their first snowboarding lesson, Sophia was feeling very worried. She didn't want to fall over in the snow and be the worst in the class. And she didn't want Robert to laugh at her. Her brother was clever and did everything better than she did.

There were ten children in the snowboarding class and their teacher's name was David. Sophia liked him because he was young and very kind. They started their lesson on a small hill, which was fine, but then David took them on the lift to the top of the mountain. All the other children followed David down the mountain but Sophia couldn't. She was too frightened. The class disappeared and Sophia was alone.

But then David came to find her. 'The others are waiting for you at the bottom,' he said. 'Come on. Be brave. I'll help you.' They went very slowly at first. Then they went a bit faster. 'You see,' said David, 'You can do it!' When she arrived at the bottom of the mountain, everyone clapped. Sophia didn't fall over once, so she felt really pleased.

'Well done!' said David. 'You didn't fall over once!'

'Wow,' said Robert. 'You looked really cool.'

'Come on. Let's have a snowboarding race,' said Sophia after their lesson. 'I can go as fast as you now!'

Examples

Sophia felt worried before her ....first............... snowboarding lesson.

Her brother Robert was always ....better............... at everything than Sophia.

Questions

1   The children's .... was called David.

2   Before the class went to the top of the mountain they practised on ....

3   Sophia was .... to follow David and the class down the mountain.

4   David helped Sophia to .... the mountain.

5   All the children clapped when Sophia got to the ....

6   Sophia was .... because she didn't fall over.

7   Sophia wanted to .... after their lesson.

Part 6

– 5 questions –

Read the email and write the missing words. Write one word on each line.

Hi George,

Example   I'm really excited about your visit ....next.............. week.

1   I hope you .... music because there will be

2   a festival here in town. It will .... great fun

because there will be some really cool bands and also a funfair.

3   .... you like pizza? We can try the new pizza

restaurant if you like. My sister says they make the nicest pizza

4   .... has ever tasted!

What time does your train arrive? All my family will be there on the

5   platform at the .... to meet you!

Harry

Part 7

Look at the three pictures. Write about this story. Write 20 or more words.

....

....

....

....

....

Blank Page

Blank Page

Speaking

Examiner's copy

Find the Differences

Candidate's copy

Find the Differences

Examiner's copy

Information Exchange

Helen's sports club

where	Long Road
when / go	Monday evenings
who / go with	sister
what / play	football
expensive	no

Oliver's sports club

where	?
when / go	?
who / go with	?
what / play	?
expensive	?

Candidate's copy

Information Exchange

Helen's sports club

where	?
when / go	?
who / go with	?
what / play	?
expensive	?

Oliver's sports club

where	Park Street
when / go	weekends
who / go with	cousin
what / play	golf
expensive	yes

Examiner's and Candidate's copy

Picture Story

The aliens go for a ride

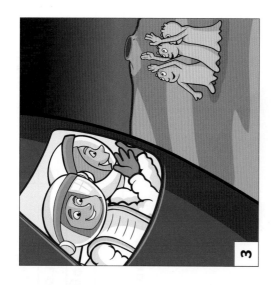

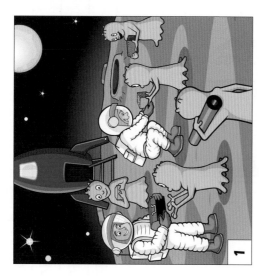

Blank Page

Examiner's copy

Find the Differences

Candidate's copy

Find the Differences

Examiner's copy

Information Exchange

Nick's favourite teacher

name	Miss Cave
subject / teach	geography
what / hobby	doing puzzles
where / live	Park Road
long / short hair	long

Jill's favourite teacher

name	?
subject / teach	?
what / hobby	?
where / live	?
long / short hair	?

Candidate's copy

Information Exchange

Jill's favourite teacher

name	Mr May
subject / teach	history
what / hobby	cycling
where / live	West Street
long / short hair	short

Nick's favourite teacher

name	?
subject / teach	?
what / hobby	?
where / live	?
long / short hair	?

Examiner's and Candidate's copy

Picture Story

A very good dog

Frank

Blank Page

Examiner's copy

Find the Differences

Find the Differences

Examiner's copy

Information Exchange

Sarah's holiday

where / go	mountains
who / with	cousins
when	January
what / buy	bracelet
what / weather like	sunny

William's holiday

where / go	?
who / with	?
when	?
what / buy	?
what / weather like	?

Candidate's copy

Information Exchange

Sarah's holiday

where / go	?
who / with	?
when	?
what / buy	?
what / weather like	?

William's holiday

where / go	beach
who / with	grandparents
when	August
what / buy	trainers
what / weather like	windy

Examiner's and Candidate's copy

Picture Story

Grandma and Grandpa come to help

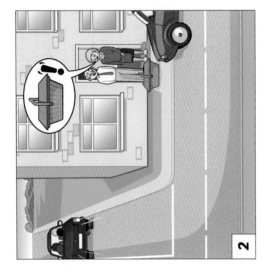

Emma   David

Blank Page

Blank Page

Blank Page

Blank Page